# Peter Jensen
# When Waves Sprout Birds

## Twenty years of poetry
## 1965–1985

In memory of my mother,
Marion Ebbers Jensen,
Teacher
1908–1981

And for my father,
William J. Jensen

Walking Bird Publishing
Eugene, Oregon

By the same author:
*This book is not a mask for tear gas* by snorkel

Many of these poems first appeared in the following periodicals:
*TriQuarterly, Redstart, Oregon Daily Emerald, Eugene Augur,
Concrete Statement, People's Planetary Almanac, 10 point 5 arts
magazine, The Anthology of Eugene Writers.*



Copies of this book may be
purchased from
Peter Jensen
Walking Bird Publishing
340 N. Grand Street
Eugene, Oregon 97402

First Edition
500 Copies

ISBN 0-9615387-0-8

Printed at Northwest Working Press
Typeset by The Production Department
Book design: Peter Jensen

PRINTED IN THE UNITED STATES OF AMERICA

# Contents

Contents (continued)

# When Waves Sprout Birds

"Don't stand there looking daggers at the sky.
You side with us and I'll make you a king
And feed you bird's milk by the bucketful!"

—Aristophanes, Birds

# The Merry-go-round

*for the memory of Gretha Olsen*

His bright paint shades to possibility.
Beneath his roof the orange stud-stallion turns
Out in that field which hesitates for quite
A while before it turns and disappears.
Some mares and colts pull carts, all nagging on
The reins, but all see through without a blink,
While followed by a lion's opened jaws.
And thump! now comes a white, fat elephant.

Just like in woods, a stag trots round the bend,
But here he's saddled and must go so slow
A little girl in blue can have her ride.

And on the lion too, a little boy
Stays on by hugging hard around its neck:
He locks his hands inside red lion's jaws.

And thump! now comes that fat white elephant.

The horses all glide by, and girls smooth down
Bright skirts and glance about. Forgetting that
These wooden horses once had gaits and names,
They flutter one free hand each time they pass.

Now thump, again here comes that elephant.

All this keeps whirling by until it's done:
An orange and a red, a white and blue and brown.
A small white profile turns to shining hair
And there a timid boy can't hide his smile.
This rider's smiling everywhere ignites
The air, and all are breathless, spending bliss
Upon this turning stage of heedlessness.

*after Rainer Maria Rilke*

## Pacific words

*for Mary Coleman*

Here surf boards flip like dolphins
as surfers fall, and waves
slide in like snow off roofs

into gutters of the Pacific here.
Say fifty gulls fly by flapping
along a single line strung there

for breakers to limbo in under growing small.
This spine of beating vertebrae signs off
its crest track, curves to thread

the hole a rock caves in the ocean's sky.
It's a single gull's tail whipped along
by many slaving wings.

The single speck goes out
against brown parch of rock.
They do not rise again.

It is assumed they're drowsing out there,
warm lids orange, heads backward,
and their bone noses pointing into feather beds.

Nude babies whip the tips of the Pacific
with tails of kelp, and there
a pair of German shepherds stops

its romping paws and humps.

Between this line and that one,
there is a swim,
my first Pacific dip

since I was seven, brave,
and learning waves in Mexico were friends
where legs and arms all mattered,

and easy water made a float of me.

As I swam out through breakers here,
humans staggered wildly on a wave,
lost it, fell, and signalled losing with

4

a big fish leaping off their heels.

Mary, they don't know it,
but everything is leaping here for you.
For you that fishing boat is rocking

over rocks and fish, for you
a double-winger banked to miss
the castle sleeping in that cliff

and circled dressed and undressed
and the surf to make us one,
but only from the sky,

for you three Black men trotted by
on strawberry speckled horses,
laughing out long purple kerchiefs,

for you two Chinese children
show me now enough feathers in their hands
to make ten birds, for you

a one-armed bearded man
flings a frisbee into the high
wind over surf. It booms up, arangs

around among the freaked-out gulls,
and slices back to where
he runs to snatch it with his only hand,

for you a motorcycle skirts the foam,
for you the clothes are coming off,
and finally, see, for you there's me,

who will stay here till the fog,
the surf of the evening, chills me,
and that single sloop the sun turns off

and scuds away for night on this gray sea.

Then I'll walk the sound of this water back
up to a lightless tunnel where I'll run
to catch a green trolley

dragging its bell along between two silver rails
up and down the city hills
where pastel houses grow among the palms.

*San Francisco*

# from Point Lobos Songs

## Coast Morning Glory

Mozartian angels
blow through me in the morning
I'm a bindweed blush
a French horn for fresh air

Other plants must put me up
My vines are weak as Botticelli hair
I play lightly on my pedicels
my leaves are angel moult

Mozart tossed around so light
the weight of one sixteenth    note

## Sand of China Beach

The cliffs are teacups breaking down to me
I'm shattering white   a wedding dress
whiter sand never met water
I'm a gentle bride in underwear

Water goes green over me
I have caves where dreams turn dark
Swim over me like water   Feel
your green turn white and break

Push my kelp flaps aside
Come into my cave
Sing love songs with me
I'll be your music woman

## Wild Buckwheat Song


I'm humble like nipples of a saint
Bees are my lovers
Jeezus they love me
They call me their clover

But I'm Buddha's buckwheat
No one really knows me
I rust when Autumn bleeds
and shake out wild buckwheat seeds



## Poison Oak Song


I like paths because I like people
I'm a pretty leaf   pity me
scratch my backside

Oils poison oils buy my oils
I'm a witch in a bush
hunched over a cackle
My chin and my nose
grew into a handle

Grab it   hold tight
My bat's teeth will bite
you'll take home the itch
in my dirty whiskers
a witch's kiss will creep
in your skin for a week

Do I sneer  do I sneak
I keep sabbaths on hillsides
My red lick is honest as honey
Sucker  scabs on your body

## Red Sea Fig Song

Rocky gardens grace Granite Point
with sea fig chief and red
among silvery green leaves and lichen
and nipply wild buckwheat

Goldenwhite granite loaves
baked with brown sugar on top
lump the sloping table to the sea
Salads and cereals rush in the eating eye

With the sea fig fingers red
like meat full of blood
like the pasty strokes Van Gogh
took out of the side of his life


## Big Sur Hawk Song

Once in a winter storm
that came up like a dream
as I was cruising Big Sur currents
humped like headlands they flow
I was blown off north

My wide black wings
were partly snapped
I plummeted like a broken boy
crashed in the grass of Carmelo Meadow

Where I stumbled sleepless
spent weeks hidden in grass
eating skinks and mice for I
could still jump in the air and pounce

While my wings knit muscle nerves
I flew into a pine and spied
like a heart pinned
in the pine tree's ribs

I wandered waves along the air
back to high Big Sur
Point Lobos never was my home
I rested there

8

## Viet Nam

Jets of jellied gas and phosphorous
saturate the countryside with running blood.

Buddha's monks keel over really orange
in nimbus animals of imitation napalm.

The crowd cries out! Flames crackle.
Satori is terror!


## The Cure of Folly

If you try to hide the fact
that you can be a fool,
it will appear
a turnip in your hair.

And then some other fool
can grip the leaves
and with his foot on your ear,
uproot the vegetable.

Then you'll try to cover
the hole with a new hair-do
and act as if you hadn't learned
a thing about yourself.

Yah, yah! a crazy streak
cuts all of us in two!

*after Jan van Stijevoort, 1524*

# Brooklyn Bridge

Hey Coolidge,
               shout for joy!
I'll also spend all my words
                      on good things in life.
Blush, you old beet,
                at my foreigner's praise.
                            Go red
as our Bolshevik flag,
                  no matter how sure you are
that the states
           of america
                  unite in you,
                        polis of glue.
As a looney old mama
               falls down
                  in a church,
or a monk shuffles off
               to a chilly  cell
                      and shuts the door,
so I,
     in scarves of river fog,
                 deep in evening,
carefully walk out
             on Brooklyn Bridge.
As a general, victorious,
                sweeps into a city
                      all smashed
among cannon with muzzles
                 stretching to see like giraffes,
so, turned on with glory,
               in love with this life,
I stride,
        proud of my steps,
                 upon Brooklyn Bridge.
As a silly painter
             plunges his eye,
so sharp and in love,
               into a museum's best madonna,
so I, close in the sky
             wired with stars,
gaze at Manhattan
             through Brooklyn Bridge.
New York,
       sluggish and foul
              until night,

has dropped
              its rush and high towers:
only
      ghosts at home
coil up
         like glowing worms
                             in windows.
Out here
           trains hum along
                             like wires in wind.
These gentle drones
                     tell me only
that trains are crawling
                          and clattering
like automat plates
                     piping hot
                                piled into racks.
While a furious cop car
                         goes straight
beneath its spinning light,
                              masts tipped
with glass stars
                   slip under the bridge
with ships,
             no bigger than pinheads.
I feel great pride in this,
                             this mile of steel:
out here
           my visions are towers.
Here's a struggle
                   for construction, not style,
a juxtaposition of stone
                          and austere steel.
If doomsday dawns
                   on this saddened world,
and chaos
           plows through our planet,
and if what's
               left over
                          will be this
bridge,
         rearing half-ruined
                              through the dust
of an almost completed
                         destruction,
then,
       as lizards a hundred feet long

are rebuilt from bones
                    finer than needles
                                    and prance
in locked-up
                monster halls of museums at night,
so,
    from bits of this bridge,
                        a hypothetical scientist
will put back together
                    our very contemporary world.
He will say:
            (I can hear him)
                            "That there paw of steel
once joined seas
                to prairies, and from
this very spot,
                Europe rushed to the West
scattering on the wind
                    Indian feathers.
This here beam
                reminds me of a kind of machine.
Just picture this:
                    would there have been enough hands,
after planting
                steel feet in Manhattan,
to yank
        all Brooklyn across
                        by the lip?
By these frizzled snakes
                        from electric cables,
I identify the era
                    after the age of steam:
here
        men
            ranted on radio!
Here
        men
            took off in planes!
For some here,
            life, as they say,
                            was swell!
Others were so damned hungry
                            they howled all their lives,
a howl so prolonged
                    people picked up the tune
in their bodies,
                turned down the lights,
                                and made jazz.

From this catwalk,
                men without work
dropped
        like wingless angels
                        down to the River.
Now, my screen
            is all clear
as I stretch it
            on strings to the toes of the stars.
I see why:
            here stood Mayakovsky,
bent over double
                making verses,
                            sound
                                    by
                                    sound.
I gape
      as an old woman gapes at a rocket!
I attack this fact
                as a tick buries its head
to suck its living
                from an animal, lumbering, vast.
Brooklyn Bridge.
Da! Da! That's a wonderful thing!"


after Vladimir Mayakovsky, 1925

# Humor

for the memory of Joseph Schoenfeld

Caesars, Czars and Presidents,
sovereigns of war, subjects of rumor,
have ordered troops to march over dissidents
but never could give commands
                    to humor.
Aesop, the hobo, a man of smiles,
inspected palaces of powerful fools,
who basked like hippos in the latest styles,
and thought them equals of graveyard ghouls.
In houses where hypocrites
                    did their dance,
Hodja Din
          with jokes and yawns
exposed their lies,
              took off their pants,
knocked down mean minds
                like a row of pawns!
They tried to commission
              a humorous work,
but humor took the gold
                and giggled.
They tried to lasso
              the joker's neck,
but humor bit the rope
              and wriggled.
It's harder than hell
              to execute humor!
They cut him off a million times.
They could from his body his grinning head sever.
On the point of a pike
              they stopped his rimes,
until the mummer's squeaky recorders
hushed cities to hear
              his comic play,
and humor shouts defiantly,
              "I'm here under orders
of a goat who makes me
              dance all day!"
In an old winter coat
              with straw sticking out,
with crocodile tears
              and a mask of repentance,
a political criminal,
            a parasite lout,

humor trudges
            to his death sentence.
He appears to harbor
                resignation,
wears heavenly hope
                as Jesus wore it,
but suddenly drops
                his coat at the station,
waves his hand,
                and makes a run for it!
Humor was locked in solitary.
That didn't protect the state from his groans,
which he sang out like a trumpet voluntary,
bright humor breaks
                through prison stones.
Coughing up phlegm like a man in the ranks,
a silly old ballad his only chalice,
he shot at cadets and spat at tanks,
his rifle aimed at the Winter Palace.
He's accustomed to hardships and gloomy ideas,
they slide off his back like a useless pack.

And sometimes his skill at panaceas
torments him himself on a ticklish rack.
He's quick,
            and he never withers away.
Nothing penetrates
                the masses as he can,
so organize
            for him today.
Humor is a brave human!


                    *after Evgeni Evtushenko*

# The terrible tail pipe flute

*for the Peace Movement*

A tail pipe flies
like a trapeze
without any strings,
and the tune it brings

is an ugly whine
because it came
from a Phantom
shot down in Nam.

The tail pipe flies
through the skies
jet propelled by
being so high.

Why do people
beneath the steeple
dive for the ground
when tail pipe's around?

Silly, stand up!
Why did you drop?
It's not the whole jet,
just the tail flute.

The tail pipe cruises
without any whosiz:
it's limitless
and pilotless.

It never comes down,
it's safe as a sound
or a tree with no root:
it's the tail pipe flute!

One rusty note
light as a mote
is all it plays
for all its days.

Why do musicians
break up positions
when that flute alert
makes a pass on their concert?

Why do school kids
jump under sewer lids
when tail pipe talk
screeches like chalk?

Why do sick reds
fall out of their beds
when visited by
the tail pipe fly?

Tail Pipe's tooting
has people shooting.
It must be very bad
music to drive them so mad!

Perhaps it's too modern,
far out or foreign.
It's very hard
to dig avant garde!

Besides it's spooky
downright creepy
to see a flute
yell and float

all on its own
like an old bone
bouncing around
all over the ground

with a bone-gnashing sound
and no dog around.
There must be a
occult sort of way

to explain the existence
of tail pipe's persistence.
Let's find the root
and stop that toot
and turn off the hoot
of that tail pipe flute!

# Wet Hawks in Oregon

*for my mother*


This fall we saw
our first wet hawks
Suddenly
a cold snap
and it's too cold to fly

They sat like oil-soaked
seagulls ducks or cormorants
on fence posts between barbed wire
their hooks and claws curved dead weights

They sat sponges
under the sea
hunched lumps of brown hawk bushes
growing in the plucked trees
like potatoes

They sat by roadside ditches
beggars wearing wet burlap
shivering
in the ruining rain

They sat grounded jets
shuddering in fits
like a tell tale feather
and their victims rabbits and mice
relieved of hawks turned to face
their other enemy the weather

# Karl's nose

*for Vickie Nelson*

Karl is a farmer of the Willamette Valley
who asked me if I'd pick his filberts
after I finished extracting honey for the Larsons,
and one thing Karl has got to be very proud of is
a wonderful long bent nose and two kind, crafty eyes!

Karl's nose is this nation's sniffling hope
as we hobble toward the '72 election.
Karl's nose is longer than our chance for peace.
I appoint Karl's nose chief U.S. peace maker in Paris!
Karl's nose being blown in a red bandana
is Nixon's visit to China.

Karl's nose is my chances for a good job
and your chances for a good job,
but enough of delaying:
let me at once wish you by Karl's nose
a warm house this winter out of the rain
and friends with you
and love if you are lucky
and at least enough food stamps to eat!

But Karl's five inch wonderful nose
is not our generation's revolution,
it is not an end to fascism in our time.
But I sure wish everybody could see Karl's nose.
It would be one good place to take aim from!

## The Seahorse Report

Seahorse has a pouch on his belly
full of small change, food and his kids.
His children, of course, are little sea horses
with monkey tails and pony heads.

Seahorse has a hide like a rasp,
a mouth like a flute and an eye like a sparrow.
He looks like a doodle when he swims past.
All this creature's features are borrowed.

Seahorse is a poet as well:
he dreams of steaming into a seaport
tall as a tanker on his tail.
This news making the evening report.

# From Songs of the Purple Planet

## I come up out of my tide pool on the purple planet

and see green crystals flash
millions of spiked lights
where they crust yellow rocks with sparks of salt
and I peer up through the pale green sky
at two oblong suns

orbiting each other
around a spaced center
the large one fire white energy
the smaller bright blue
where orange fountains leap to loop to fall

and I howl like a two-legged coyote
for the browns and greens and blues of earth
but then the twin suns turn purple and set
Twelve moons come up screaming ice
and swallow my howl


## Poetry is wonderful it can go anywhere

*for David, Judy and Ariel Sachter-Zeltzer*

because here I can say that this trail up through the woods
is the same excitement at every turn
as finding my lovers orgasm and mine like finding
a flower Ive never seen or like kneeling
to tickle a fairy slipper orchid under its chin

which is the same pleasure I get from searching
through this poem and finding a black and yellow striped
swallowtail butterfly here fly out of these lines
Let it go flap-doodling made out of words
a phantasmagoria in the air

and then all of a sudden war breaks into my poem
The Middle East cries out like a shot dove
Israeli school children die and Palestinians too
are strafed down by Israeli jets and this poem
that began so openly closes with tears

## Song of the shearwaters


Our dory jumps across the roll at Yaquina Bay bar
out past Newports two ocean splitting rock jetties
and into the remains of last nights fog banks
heading southwest on the compass rose for salmon
Our boat hammers on waves like someone

groping for details of a dream thats drowning
Thats when we see dark gray bits floating in fog
that hang like pieces of a slow exploding world
shearwaters that glide within troughs
and flap rapidly to slip over the tops of swells

gray round-tailed open-beaked birds that fish
by searching for anchovies and herring along
the rip tide line that upwells full of life
We slow down in this bird world and like a shearwater
lower our trolling poles and follow this lucky rip


## Song of the ladder of fish


On the sea bottom off Yaquina Bay flutter giant halibut
and goggle eyed ling cod yawn for bait
while the spiney brown rock bass pouts at its bright
orange cousin red snapper who scoots aside
to let a dog fish shark twist by and then

there are the brown white bellied clouds of hake
and a middle school of narrow mackerel   In the green
upwelling cool waters coho silver salmon
and king chinooks go looking for the Alsea River
finding lures and millions of silver bait fish on the way

These herring and anchovies fling from salmon
Further out in warmer oceanic current
double ended albacore shoot under waves
An occasional twenty foot basking shark pokes his nose
among gray whales going over and under along the coast

## Whale whale

Out off Alsea River floating over the Rock Pile
salmon fishing grounds below us at twenty-five fathoms
we hear a womans voice scream on the radio
—Help Weve hooked a whale And we see a white dory
rock violently tip almost over a mile away

The woman explains over the airwaves—A gray whale
grabbed a flasher on our gear bent the pipe davit down
to the water nearly tipped us over We cut
the line with wirecutters After the days fishing
I meet her in a hardware store in Newport buying new gear

The man behind the counter grins with broken teeth
—Ive known whole boats to go over and lose all
because some forty foot gray whale cant stand the itchy
barnacles on his back so he scrapes them off with a small boats keel
Thatll be fifty dollars That was a cheap whale


## A poet should go out there

and keep going like a surfer
We re never coming back anyway
so keep getting better stronger
richer in ways of the worlds waves
even if blue sharks crisscross under your board

Be like a surfer looking for new breakers
new curls new pipelines
to shoot through new curved slopes to plane along
and if the wave or poem doesnt build right
wheel over the top and walk out on water

where the flat sea lets you wait
for the next poem or wave the ocean brings in
and then get up get up and fly
Feel the dolphin under your feet
Forget matter   Focus on energy

**I backpacked many miles looking for something**


a wild orchid a pool of tad poles salmon leaping
skunk cabbage bear shit a meteor shower
two fawns waggling their ears
a raccoon choking a frog
gold flies Ollalie Creek under snow

a cougar taking down a doe
both screaming in a cloud of dust
two golden eagles carving a canyon with their cries
a line of quail running along in sage brush
and all these things

it took to uncover my eyes
and make up for one blinding event
that happened on the purple planet
a person named America
whose mind broke in two and drifted apart



**One day on the purple planet a saucer landed**


out came green lizard creatures with hot pants on
with cactus horns flowering on their heads
They grabbed me with octopus suckers on their tails
and dragged me inside their glowing spaceship
that hovered like a huge crab with lights inside

—We are taking you to our planet as an experiment
came out of the mouths of my guard
who smelled like low tide at Coney Island
and I woke up in the USA in the 1950s
with Joe McCarthy stabbing his fingers at me

and Dick Nixon slobbering over me like a cocker spaniel
while Elvis got his pelvis shot down in Korea
and cops and pilots were sighting flying saucers
I tried to hide between Jane Mansfields breasts
but a draft board began counting off my pimples

## Sing a song of Robert Bly

who out of the open door of Odin House sings
translations from the Swedish and other dances
He has his farmhouse on his head like a helmet
and is greatly influenced by Carol Bly
and the Great Mother the kids and a three year old son

Who was that Native American knight Neruda
who rode by on horseback with the Chilean junta
wriggling on the obsidian tip of his spear
Dragons will be dragons until doomsday Poets know
so they speak from inside ancestor heads like monkey warriors

When the Great Mother yells for more pearls like Liz Taylor
and Big Duke Daddy John Wayne directs the Vietnam War
from the set of a phoney barroom while the whole world
hears war orphans wail blessed be people
who balance between nipples wise hearts


## Do you wonder how Vietnamese

survived such bombing year after year
They had to find a way
to live in tunnels
without being shell-shocked by B-52s
that flew over Nam pounding the ground

from ten thousand feet every day
The bombardier pushed a button by his scope
while the crew drank coffee or gin on the run
between Okinawa and Thailand while Vietnamese
ran into tunnels put plugs in their ears

and climbed into hammocks hung on posts
by thick bands of rubber so they would bounce
with earth-thundering concussions and survive
anything but a direct hit and come back up
ready to fight or heal or farm

## The Morse Ranch is a small state at peace


with a white house and green swings for grandchildren
Wayne Morse shouldve been President since 1963
this old Eugene place says to me
When Joe and I went to interview the Senator
we waited under an immense big leaf maple tree

and an old cowboy from John Day Ranch
took time from mowing the lawn to say with a grin
—Waynes harder to get hold of than a fart in a skillet
Now the Senator his red cattle and his horse are gone
I walked in a stand of oaks   They were like long

shadows of anti-war demonstrators waving leafy hands
Below the house in spreading blackberry vines
I came upon a herd of twelve black-tailed deer
American gazelles does fawns and a spike buck
sweet nervous deer inside protection of this ranch



## Wedding song for Dong and Phuong


Dear Vietnamese friends sister and brother woman and man
we send you our love from Eugene urgently written
as if for a leaflet but in happiness for your wedding
on the West Coast of America a country we love
as dearly as you love Viet Nam

We want the marriage of Peace and the Paris Agreement
we who might have met without the war
at a world-wide conference sailing in like seabirds
to an island in the middle of the Pacific
running around raising our UN wings and songs

Instead we carefully celebrate and plan
one year after one third of a terrible air force
was shot from the sky by people of Hanoi and Haiphong
we who have marched together for the political prisoners
with whom we share so many hopes Phuong and Dong

# After hawks sailed away

leaving blue air clear
a tan wood dove rapidly beat its wings
to cross the river from one clump of trees
to another and disappear
trailing a flight plan of fear

In brush gold finches twittering stopped
and small brown birds with blue heads jumped
up branch by branch to look around
and whistle a warning to all wings
whose silence made the river mutter more

It must have been like this in Minneapolis
when a great horned owl landed on a bridge
when poets looked up and said —It must be John
Berryman coming back to check out this town
from the bridge where he threw his body down


# A pyramid of sulphur 1973

*for men of the Poling Bros tanker fleet*

Clotted yellow powder stands fifty feet high
by a steel shovel and conveyor belt lumped with snow
The air is runny with fumes as a passenger jet
intensifies its kerosene whistles roars its take off slant
and leaves earth through yellow haze miles away

Cracking towers float beneath the smoked sun
Pipes and catwalks climb all over them   Steam and fumes
escape uncoil and spin until even solid oil tanks
wobble and swim like oil drums wallowing in the wake
of a super crude oil tanker leaving the refinery

Suddenly the air blows up and blobs of flame
shoot like comets and engulf men whole as they run
Flaming gas gushes out and lights the sulphur pyramid
Black smoke from New Jersey
Forty-one oil workers died this February

## Distracted love song

I kiss her fingertips and think of Victor Jara
his fingers cut off singing for popular unity
and I go on kissing her everywhere
on all her soft parts her mouth tongue ears
nipples and the orchid around her clitoris

to protect all our soft parts from harm
especially the small of her back her eyelids
and between her breasts on her heart
I will go on kissing her sweet cheeks belly button
folds behind her knees while receiving her kisses

I go on thinking of a broken guitar in Chile
holding all of her and folk singer Victor Jara inside me
He sang till the Army machine-gunned him   Then such silence
So I ll sing of my lover and this poet with no fingers
with my breath ink tears sperm and spit of this song


## Song to make you happy in winter

*for Alison Loren Halderman*


Heres a funny poem   Color it half yellow half green
See its a wool sock with no holes   No its two wool socks
Hey put this green and yellow poem on your feet
and dance around on the cold wood floor
Swing your arms and jump up jump up

Two wool socks six inches up off the floor then
run around like rabbits at dawn
among sage bushes   Their noses quiver
like buttons tied to a tree of nerves
Hush there are two socks hopping across the floor

Up in the nerve tree sits a pair of ringnecked mittens
cooing   Now color this poem cool dove tan
but theres a warm light coming on
Put the doves on your hands and fly up
into soft sunlight   Hi you are high

## Writing dialogue haikus with my friend

*also for Alison*


is my favorite game is like lighting matches
I write of water breaking light into pieces
She writes of ripe persimmons hanging over water
I write of orange feelings and orange tasting kisses
She writes of fires that burn inside and out

We play cards and we play chess
but haikus is the game we play best
interweaving consciousness
that dances into her and into me
like a spirit caught in the persimmon tree

Great wind protect my younger friend
and protect my mind
We are only haikus in the human storm
Let us love and both grow
Calm our dreams   Turn our purples orange


## The flowers of bear grass are like a white torch


Leaves of trillium taste richer than lettuce
Wild strawberries sweeten the picking backpackers way
into wilderness green turning on after most of the snow
snuck away in creeks to march down rivers
and at last Mink Lake swells up like a blue pillow

Later as the full moon climbed on Packsaddle Mountain
and our little fire was the afterburner of a rocket
sunk deep in the earth like a diver from the stars
a bear sang its grunt and growl song and we two
huddled by our crashed spaceship and fed it sticks

The evenings mosquitos were gone with drops of our blood
as her period tugged at the moon on the mountain
and the bear song made us gather flare-up branches
and make thick clubs with burning heads crawl into the fire
as the bear followed its spring growl and the moon over
        the mountain

## Who is in the mountains

when snow crosses the sky like a dragon of white wind
and circles peaks unsettling everything
that humans find to cling to
when witnesses are glaciers that crack
and crunch down on a shelf of crumbled lava

Who is in the lightning that breaks into branches
as it splits through mountain passes
as its flashes reveal shoulders of snow
rock faces miles of grey distance low
pointy black forests and formless explosions of clouds

Who is in the wind that rebels against mountains
that blows snow and lightning up ridges
flows over and between broken walls
from the ocean up through winters fortress
Its no one   The belly of all legends


## Three interlocking poems   Volcano


## A white dog drank from blue Spirit Lake

chased Harry Trumans cats around his lodge
pissed on a gas pump in Toutle ran down
Toutle River past a logging camp sniffed
at young campers making love in a sleeping bag
growled at a geologists black dog

raised his leg against the tallest doug fir
ran over rumbling earth eagerly
chased a doe and her new fawn back uphill
looked out over the watershed of Toutle and Cowlitz
down to the Columbia and a ship loaded with Hondas

took one last drink from the volcanos reflection
on Spirit Lake howled at everything in sight
dribbled on ashes of a recent camp fire just so
ran once around the lake climbed to timberline
and disappeared into white void of snow

## Mount Saint Helens myths

drift across the Northwest like cloud fronts
Don Lelooska recalls that Saint Helens was
a beautiful princess with sharp breasts loved
by Mount Adams and Hood both steaming for her
But neither could win her   She played them

against each other   They fought for centuries
all three of them yelling at once sending up smokes
Three passionate mountains were too much for Coyote
that funny little dog god who was everywhere
They troubled his naps made him cough

covered his stomping grounds with miles of ash
Worst of all made his yips sound little and silly
So he arranged the Columbia to separate Mount Hood
had angry Mount Adams blow his brains out
and covered the woman with a robe of snow until


## Mount Saint Helens tears open the earth

to reveal the purple planet over sixty dead
firs flattened for fifteen miles
a ten megaton blast to warn all kids
born since Hiroshima and the Test Ban Treaty
about fine points of ash jet stream and fallout

People cough in Eugene joke about the pollen count
while spooky ash dusts cars   Only old people
and a Japanese woman put on dust masks
The volcano up north is now a black caldera
with a hot oval dome inside like Wizard Island

It will be rebuilding for decades reminding
us we have been here for half a second
Portland may not be the best place for a city
and other minor lessons like Trojan and Timberline Lodge
Definitely the mountain comes from a different time zone

## Linten Springs waterfall is a trip


a movie of wildflowers and water up to dry rock
into the brain of the wilderness
Start at purple lupines and Paynes gray rocks
Climb to a zone of orange paintbrushes violet stars
yellow winks waved by leaves over tufty mossheads

Theres my bird brother the dipper bopping at me
From a log he flies into a pool plops
under bubbling cool   I hold my breath for him Ouzel
He pops up sends vibrations from his eye
and flies away over rich tree wreckage water eats

Climb up logs to terraces of showering rims and dripped slime
Look up into a half funnel of rocks and pumice dust
where pink penstemons wave like hands stuck on a cliff
Climb high to look down far but under a little pine
hummingbird visits air before my face and blurs my dream



## Song of rufous hummingbird


This feels like first day of spring warm flowering
Something is chip chip chipping pieces off silence
There in red quince bush speedy
golden bronze floating thumb with day glo nail
bzee bzee bzee rufous hummingbird male

Zip zap zoop on the way from Mexico to Canada
to mate hovers here sips from cherry and quince
Hey whered he go that hitch-hikers thumb
who migrates with the warm front opening north
Up there in bare budding tree   V-v-vrip dives wheee

down to sexy thicket with bees   Bzee
bzee bzee   Tiny buzzer rings
insistently centers the afternoon sings
vibrates flash back   Flower visitor for sweet water
lightens up time with his whir-working wings

## Once youve seen Saturn

through a telescope part of your head is out there
circled by rings spaced out with that cosmic monster
That far out piece of your head orbits a solar
nucleus tilted this way and that deep yellow gas ball
with crazy rainbow dusted rings

What is Saturns influence   Does it return
Did its weird shape launch flying saucers
magnetic heavy cruising through stations
of fire circle stonehenge zodiac
Is it the crown and aura of the golden age

I remember how Saturn fell into my right eye
big as the moon through a tube aimed from a shipyard
owned by the grandson of the man who built
the first submarine Nautilus which sat there on blocks
a huge wood barrel with hand cranks washed by starlight


## Night song in the universe

Last night I went skin diving in outer space
nothing but darkness wrapped around me
Stars circled my fingers like rings
Stars tickled my toes   Pointy stars made me sneeze
and gave me star fever as they went up my nose

Three bright stars burned into my sex
One struck my bellybutton ooof
Two stars settled on my nipples like medals
A mouthful of stars made me yell to silence space
but stars sat in my ears to piccolo

O o two stars are headed for my eyes
Im too far out   Something out here
is trying to make me a constellation
Its time I landed on the purple planet
where I can hide inside my shadow

## Egg song

Up in the World Tree
sits the Great World Chicken
afraid of the World Serpent
who would eat her Eggs.

One day, when the Eagle of the Sky
and the Serpent of the Sea
were doing battle,
the Great Hen successfully hatched out
a Big Egg filled with
the plenty species of the World.

And they all ran away
from sounds of the tremendous battle
to find peaceful harbors, valleys, coves
and meadows to live and brood in.

Later Eggs with more good stuff in them
were eaten by the Serpent,
and the Hen was devoured by the Eagle.
So, we were very lucky to get as much in the World
as we have got. Think of that!

> *after a story told me by my*
> *Danish Grandmother,*
> *Margrethe Korsgaard Jensen,*
> *Bedstemor from Skjern*

# First Meeting with Aliens

*for Ursula LeGuin*


Once barefoot on a dark night
I was walking along a Long Island dirt road,
jumpy, happy, when I bumped
into a feathery thing
and fell on my back as it flapped
in my face and covered stars with four wings.

Yow! I howled like a hound
about to be carried off
to an eagle's nest on Mars.

What I had bumped into
was two blue herons mating!
Interrupted, mama and papa
blue heron took off for space
in a break in trees overhead—
wide wings with fans separate as fingers,
scaley legs like snakes to feel,
beaks on vine necks driving up—
what a great escape!

Now, whenever I'm flat on my back
down in the world, I shout:
—Come back, wonderful aliens,
come back!

# from Songs of Cape Arago

*for Jerry and Lynn Rudy*

## Song of the creatures at dawn

Turn over stones,
look into tide pools,
consider protein-rich sea foam
whipped into egg white
meringue by waves.
If you had to create
creatures of tidal zones
mostly of sea water,
what would you make?
Creatures at Cape Arago
make me think of the sea
as if it were Sandy Calder
sculpting a circus from scraps.

# Parade of magic names

Er, here comes the nudibranch, slow-
ly, goose-necked barnacles
and their cousins the little volcanoes
who comb tides like ladies and men
comb their hair wondering about love.
Here come tube worms, cockles, anemonies,
cottids, crabs, chitons and blennies,
the sun star and its delicious urchins,
orange or purple starfish, turban snails,
limpets and shrimp, mussels,
fancy spaghetti worms, octopus and perch,
sea cucumbers, sea lettuce and eel grass,
skinny pipe fish and kelp.
Butter clams open and clap.
Black oystercatchers whistle.
Gulls and cormorants stand still
at sunset. Diving ducks pass by
gray whales undersea, as sleepy rows
of harbor seals and pups rest,
while elephant seals and sea lions
bounce the sun like a foggy pearl
from nose to nose to nose.
These waves of variety prove
ocean's ability to fiddle around.

# Coyote

*for Barre Toelken*

Coyote trots among
sandhill cranes with his tongue
hung out pretending he isn't hungry,
while he looks for a stupid big bird
to bite by the legs,
but cranes are all eyes
high up on stalks
who fly away laughing like frogs.

Scrawny coyote
grins through his teeth
after chasing an elk calf
and having been outrun sits down
to face elk bull and cow
who turn their tan rumps
at coyote and fart.

Horny coyote
stuck with snapping at mice.
The little guy says, "Hee hee,"
makes up a big story
each time he gets socked on the nose:
"Listen, there was this Indian princess
bathing in a blue-green lake,
and there was gold in the stream,
big flakes of it
where she stepped barefoot!"

What a joke, coyote,
your thinking up tricks
to burn off bear's tail,
starting a war
no one could finish.
Is that why you yip at the moon
like war dead nutty at night,
your eyes full of looney glints?

Nature made you
to laugh at itself,
little flea-bitten
American wolf,
target on the run,
coyote!

## The assassination of Peter French,
## Oregon cattle baron, 1897

Pete French fell from his saddle
with a bullet in his head like a new idea,
and seven hundred thousand cattle
mooed as if they never did believe.

West of Blitzen River Pete's blood
dried up in lava dust.
Sixty black vultures in cotton woods
above the flames of the P. Ranch house

drifted like paper ash
to judge Ed Oliver in Burns
innocent despite his smoking gun,
because Pete French rode out to take

back riparian rights where Harney Lake
was changeable to grass or swamp
as settlers, cows and birds
laid eggs among the laws

and P. Ranch canals
of Malheur Marsh.
Later in Frenchglen,
a piano tinkled at the inn

and delighted visitors ran out to see
sandhill cranes
dance Spring sex
like exiled Paiutes in the marsh.

## Salmon Redds

In one of the few quiet places in Horse Creek,
where two parts of that stream meet,
where a little gravel island grown over
with light green hands of colt's foot
divides the stream, speeds up the main flow
and diverts some in a curve that is slow,
lies gravel spawning grounds
of an eighteen member tribe of salmon.

Below these redds the creek is still slow.
Sandy shallows and rocks in the middle
or big rocks that hang over and have
water scooped-out channels under them
make a waiting place for bruised white
salmon to rest in before each hen
goes to her ancient nesting place
to lay her brilliant orange and pink roe,
the color of salmon meat smoked,
the color of wet, split cedar,
the color of salmonberry flowers, a color
reproduced by some wild roses, sunsets and salmon,
jellied eggs that trout would eat
if trout were this far up Horse Creek
from the hatchery. But only salmon
cruise these pools, and they are dying.

Even so, males, with white-striped backs
and white tails, their dorsal fins a rotten white,
chase each other, curl around, splash with fury,
compete until the last moment to win the right
to join a hen upstream and lose his fluid
over exposed, invaluable roe
held in their jelly like ripe, red huckleberries.
The males swim, circle, raise their sharp beaks
and eyes from the water to look upstream.
They see forks of Horse Creek
coming down at them and the island of colt's foot.
They see the beach on the left
and exposed rocks on the right.

This is their sacred place,
where they spent their first silver summer.
This pool is the only parent they have known.
They remember the smell of this place,
the way this water tastes in their heads.
They remember starting out with more than eighteen.
They remember how insects tumbled out of the sky
to dot the silver surface of their world.
They remember surrendering this place
to follow the flow through blind pours
into larger veins of green water.
They remember their first taste of salt,
the joining of tribes in the deep
and switching from insects to eating small fish.
They remember four years of growth,
some to three pounds, some to more than twenty.
They remember the long swim out and back
on the big island bend to Russia,
and all of this flooded back to them this Fall
when, somehow, their bodies in the ocean
changed, and they got the Cascade Mountain call.

They tasted bitter silt of Mount Saint Helens,
but didn't forget their course in the Columbia.
They hugged the north shore, to avoid
nuclear plant effluent local people say,
dodged harbor seals, sea lions and gill netters
losing great numbers in the lower Columbia,
turned right into the Willamette
and swam through Portland. Swam the sad river
from Portland through farms and turned left
at the McKenzie for Springfield mill smell,
passed mills and found sweeter McKenzie water,
fought their way up rapids and EWEB fish ladders
splitting off from other schools of salmon until
a sudden, certain taste

of Horse Creek poured over them,
and the last few aimed themselves,
darted, fought, flew up through
shallow rapids, up small falls
to their birth pool, bringing back
their exciting lives to this long bowl
of rocks set in crystal water.

They are no longer silver sides,
no longer metalic and healthy.
Besides bone white bruises, their color
is dull red or green or yellow.
It hurts to see them.
They are like older parents,
who we remember young, but in salmon
the loneliness of not bearing live young,
of dying in order to bring life back
to this fragile roadside pool in logging country,
drives us humans back down in our cars
to wonder at life as the cold returns,
as we feel the same forces that drive
salmon driving us.


Fall

for her

After whistling cedar waxwings
have wheeled away into the silver sky,

after clouds have fallen face down
and press gray bodies on green ridges,

I long for you like summer,
and I'm burned by rain.

# Kaye Turner runs with the deer

Nearby Camp Sherman
in all that beauty
from Black Butte Ranch
to the spring that opens
earth like a caesarian
birthing the Metolius,

from meadows where Three Sisters
look like three white mares
to blue Wizard Falls
where hatchery trout
suck up flies, from families
camping around a fire
where faces look strange
like black and orange masks,
to strong Kaye Turner
jogging off in blue and yellow
swooshing Nike shoes, shorts
and T-shirt, never
finishing her run.
She left an open wound
to rival the Metolius Spring.

There's no difference
between nuns raped and shot
in El Salvador by right wing
national guardsmen
and a Lane County health worker
assaulted at Camp Sherman
with only her lower jaw bone
and empty running shoe found.

Sometimes when I visit there
I mistake ponderosa sunlight,
a bounding mule deer tan,
for the spirit of Kaye Turner on the run.

## Mass in El Salvador

The Archbishop of El Salvador
was shot down saying mass,
and many people turned out for
his funeral, but Chaos

sent its death squads too and shot
into the crowd who crushed
each other as the bullets flew.
Even flowers rushed

away and stained the ground,
and no one but a weeping nun
and the bodies hung around.

# Giordano Bruno

Giordano Bruno made a fire
in sixteen hundred as he burned,
a human torch, a heretic:
the church stood still. Earth turned.

We owe this flame in Italy
the name of a crater on the moon
facing away from the human race
and one pure cry from a common loon.

Bruno talked too freely then
of atoms and planets trapped by stars,
so place his brilliant memory
in a hole bombed out by meteors.

Giordano Bruno burned at dawn
among his ignorant fellow men,
who closed their robes against the cold
and double-crossed themselves back then.

# El Salvador



As a young man you met
Otto Rene Castillo
"a drunk poet wandering in the street
full of wine and wit of a wise parrot,"
who (you were shocked to read
in my book) died spread-eagled
in the Andes under sun blades
gleaming off sunglasses of soldiers.

In 1962 your teenaged brother
got caught by soldiers
with strips of paper that read,
"Fidel Si, Yanquis No!"
and a pot of glue melted
from hooves of dead horses.
Soldiers made your brother
sit on the curb and drink
that whole pot of glue.
You watched surgeons
at San Salvador hospital
cut him open and wash
glue from his stomach lining
with surgical sponges,
and he lived with a scar
on his belly like a zipper.

Your chubby little sister grew up
into a dark Maya princess
with blue black Indian hair,
a Maya nose long as a finger,
deep brown eyes, and breasts
so soft in her white wedding blouse
they made you dream of clouds.
Her wise guy husband became
Minister of the Interior
and told you many terrible things
about Nicaraguan dictator Somoza.

Your brother-in-law
went down to the railyards to accept
a gift "from a widow in Seattle
to the people of El Salvador:"
three box car loads of boxes
wrapped in green and white
Georgia Pacific plastic.
What a wise-cracker he was
your brother-in-law of the Interior
of El Salvador! He took
out his pen knife and cut into one
of those boxes and found:
30,000 38-inch riot sticks!
Clowning for the foreign media,
he took out one club, bent over
and said:   "How thoughtful!
But our people are not so short.
These are too short for hoe handles!"

# Harald the Landwaster

Yaroslav the Wise,
cunning Russian King at Kiev,
sent Harald, the heir
to Viking Norway's throne,
down the Dnieper River
with five hundred warriors
to join the emperor's
Byzantine Varangian guard.

The stout prince stared
at the slanting copper roofs
of many-faceted
Constantinople.
His black swan ships
swept red webbed feet
toward that metal city.

There's at least one shadow
for every source of light,
and Harald was to cast
many shadows among Arabs,
Bulgars, Sicilians, Normans,
Danes, and one low shadow last:

with an arrow in his throat
near York in England as his men
exhausted the king's
and set the stage
for the Bayieu Tapestry
and William the Bastard
to end the Viking age.

*after King Harald's Saga*

# The Tempest

*for Florence E. Johnson,*
*bird lady of Quisset*

In 1602 Shakespeare's patron,
Earl of Southampton, gave aid
to Bartholomew Gosnold,
who sailed from Falmouth, England

to New England in a small bark
with thirty-two men and built
a fort on a tiny island in the pond
on the west end of Cuttyhunk,

Westernmost island in the chain
of Elizabethan Islands that dangle
off the heel of Cape Cod.
Ariel may have been a bright native boy,

the opposite of a bosun named Caliban.
Did Ariel know how to lure striped bass
by plucking tail feathers from dreaming birds
to tie onto English hooks?

Cuttyhunk is a bird lover's island
that floats like a glass egg in a storm.

# From Twenty-seven Views of Japan

*for Alan and Christine McCullough*

1.  The wind and Japanese prefer
    a trunk jagged as lightning.
The way exposed pines grow
or flowers are arranged
in an eggshell bowl:
passion bent.

2.  Buddha's garden
    is a gravel sea
raked into rows of waves
around black rock islands
that shine like zen asteroids.

3.  Two pheasants sit cris-crossed
    on one branch, one red and silver, male,
the other brown and gold, female.
The branch reaches zig-zag ways
around these mates and offers here bare twigs
and there a cluster of white flowers.
It is golden evening light in early spring
five hundred years ago right now.

4.  An entertaining laugh
    splashes from the mouth
of the comic's friend, but
the comic does not laugh:
he grimaces.

5.  Ribbons in the wind
    wonderfully
confuse me
like ribbons in women's hair.

6.      A dragon guards the rooftop
        from whatever flies around:
falcons of the enemy
sent to strike down incoming
or outgoing messenger pigeons.
The dragon's a blown up carp
with open mouth, a monster
of the deep imagination
where we see beings that we need.
The dragon's like a winding path,
the entrails of evolution,
a dinosaur wreck misunderstood,
a beast worthy to guard
whatever we're worth
as we encircle the world.

7.      A Tokyo professor
        of nuclear physics
and subatomic nonsense
stands with a tall plastic bag
on his head to spoof
masters of nothingness.

8.      Blue beauties on a wall,
        two blue love birds
sit on a limb
perched opposite
breast to breast
and do what we call kiss.
The air around them is gold.
They were frozen for
a sentimental emperor.

9.      Hokusai prints the world,
        records it fondly with goodbye
in every view. He begins
in basic blue,
the color of our water planet
and enters all other colors
like minor characters:
who play with their hats
while choosing who to love,
chase money or food,
run away from disasters
and sip tea
soon as history permits.

## Clam, starfish and worm

Before life found forms
in water or clay
the world ocean surrounded
a single continent

almost bare as the moon.
Life cooked in hot springs
lasered by nude sun rays,
spilled from pools on high tides

to float like jellied snow flakes
in surf, tried all the angles,
changed prototypes, divided, died,
became almost numberless, survived.

Bits that sank into mud
tried three routes to the future:
soft bodies, radial symmetry
and enclosed, joined segments.

Three branches fanned
out from source spots
from ur types that led
to clam, starfish and worm.

Clam climbed high as snail.
Starfish fed on clams
and tried out many points.
Worm was most progressive.

It became segmented shrimp and crabs.
It came ashore and hid in dirt.
It turned into the successful insect.
Most of life is worm's child.

## Footprints

*for Iris Kay*


The earliest discovery of dinosaur footprints
was not by a bearded expert of European geology
but by Pliny Moody in 1802, a local farm boy
near South Hadley, Massachusetts

in the valley of the Connecticut River
where red sandstone beds of the early Jurassic
lay exposed. Ornithopods roamed that valley,
herbivores on hind legs. Sometimes

they crawled on all fours. Dinosaurs were unknown
in 1802, so people thought they were the tracks
of huge birds! Some even suggested
they were the prints of Noah's raven!

Here's to Pliny Moody, pioneer,
and to all of us who discover the world!


## The discovery of anti-biotics


Why doesn't soil crawl
with harmful bacteria
and infect animals?

(Since so many sick animals
lie down on the earth and die.)

A sharp question in 1939:
"Why is soil so clean
of infectious germs?"

Answered:   molds
in soil prey upon them.
Molds can be made
into medicine.

## One fifth of all mammals are bats

Nocturnal like rats
the nightshift of bats
takes over the sky
from the birds.

These are the mammals,
not man or camels,
that sucked dinosaur eggs
from sundown to dawn

and gave lizards jitters
with high shrieks and flitters
that brought Tyranosaur Rex
to his knees.

Thanks to winged mice
and rodents not nice:
the slow oppossum,
quick weasel and rat,

the world was picked clean
of king lizard and queen
and viewed without hypocrisy,
made safer for democracy.

# Swallows

*for Brendan McCullough, bird boy*

With long, curved wings swept back,
rough-winged swallows sail
above like aboriginal
boomerangs skimmed at insects.

Think about swallows awhile
they become weird and real:
little lizards in feather suits,
condors the size of mice,

day bats without sonar or teeth,
bead eyes, hollow struts, bits of meat
stretched on a glider frame,
wire perched twittering machines,

feathery whistles in a row,
dragonflies from birdland,
imitation flying fish,
miniature pterodactyl softies,

birdbrains light as a garden pea,
speedo divers cutting up the air,
winged mysteries eating mosquitos,
escaped strokes of calligraphy,

life forms from the arms of trees,
eggs that learned to fly by falling
from their birthplace on a cliff.
So much from wondering about swallows!

# Autumn night

As the moon full of light
subdued stars and flooded
wispy clouds with silver,
a V of honkers from the north

cried out like sailors in the dark
and slowly crawled, like flies
on a dark ceiling, with wing beats
into frosty moonlight.

There they hung and honked
like the wake of some huge force,
as if a god or spaceship passed.
They tugged at all invisibles

invented, flying from our minds.
But they were geese from Canada
following a full moon mothership
who beamed their escape route south

over valleys of Oregon and wrinkled
silver lakes floating in the dark
like ports. Their wild cries fell
like angels barking for joy!

But these were mortal bird shouts
to their lead navigator, who pulled
them along with soft wings, two long strings
of fishing gear to catch our hearts.

One day, as crabbers      stood on docks

waiting for dungeness      to crawl
on fishheads wired      into their rings,
a sealion, known      to beg for trash
beside unloading      trawlers, lunged

right up onto      a floating dock
among crabbers      and tried to look
like an old man      in a rubber coat
and tried to control      its shivering.

The dulled crabbers      were astounded
by this sealion      joining them,
but understood      when a black nose rose
from Yaquina Bay      followed by

jaws of rounded      ivory pegs,
white chin, a snort,      and a cyclops eye:
the gleaming head      of a killer whale
was looking for      its slippery meat.


Like a far away lover

the snow coated volcano shines
across a complicated sea of firs.
Blue air races between us
like a symphony written in exile.

*Both of these poems are for Bill Nelson, chemist,*
*who led a tour of Forgeron Vineyard in Elmira, Oregon*


## White wines


White wines are easier:
one squeeze, and juice goes into the vat
to think over summer with a friendly batch of yeast.
White wines are more confident, like Vivaldi
played by pros. They wait in seagreen bottles
for someone who wants to relive summer.

Out pours sunlight into round glasses
to celebrate fish that slip across our plates
or fowl that tiptoe on our tables.
White wine cleans mouths
like cleared sensations between bites.

White wine shines like the sun,
that great farmer, our star.

# Red wines

Red wines are full of moods.
The squeeze must be just right.
The cake of skins and seeds
must not be pressed dry.
There are bitter things
better left to ferment in the vat
with red juice than to be
brought out right away.

There are considerations to mull,
multiple tastes to blend,
several calculations to run
before red juice is poured
into oak barrels to talk with wood.
Red wine is more like blood,
easily spilled before thoughtfulness
replaces suspicion or anger.

But like peace,
good red wine is worth the wait.
Its individuality comes
from good decisions and patience.
Its pleasure washes over
rich foods like pasta or beef.

It mellows our powers,
moderates our fears
of being only mortal fools
faced with a cosmos run down by stars
blowing themselves apart.

## Mozart's Musical Joke

Six musicians dressed in skyblue T-shirts
tiptoe into Davies Concert Hall in San Francisco.
Three men all wear silver cloudy wigs with pony tails.
One woman violist pushes out a blue balloon
T-shirt pulled over her very ready pregnancy.

They remind me of wading willets chased by waves
and dogs down at the Pacific beach,
their dainty steps interrupted, their wings
of black and white bars raised, about to fly.

Four string players hurry up, as two French horns
wind down out of tune, and all sip purple wine
as their bright wood or brass playthings rest.
The double bassist spins his wooden Willendorf

like a gleaming pregnant planet just for laughs.
The dogs are arfy on the beach, their tongues
loll and waggle like pink rococo ribbons
lovers liken to the oral surf of sex.

Mozart got goofy and child-like in 1787
to cheer up after his dear father Leopold died,
and wrote pleasurably disordered jokes
that stumble like puppies in the surf

that ran after willets and got waves in their faces
as the willets escaped like true Mozart
on light and dark wings over troubled,
white, air-bubbled broken waves
that make quick moments come and pass.

Willets wander along the California coast
in early Spring like hungry music,
wound up treble clefs that poke for shrimp,
as ocean's orchestra concludes winter's stormy coda.

Willets stand like long-stemmed wine glasses,
long-billed doohickeys on the wet mirror sand,
double jerky, wind-up twittering toys
that tease waves and make dogs clown.

Mozart's sextet floats along like a glass island
in thin air, pulls off gags that dazzle
as a violinist catches up his cadenza,
goes over the top of his run and derails,

like a high aria suffering attacks of base clef vertigo,
or lopsided, loud solos with no back up harmonies,
or a silly climax with no foreplay,
or a race to the finish that repeats

so often it's endless, or a sudden end
that leaves all six musicians turning pages
to find more notes. Mozart grins,
then giggles as his skilled clowns bow.

All this musical confusion produces magic acts:
willets spring from coiled French horns,
erect dogs dance on hind legs around the double bass,
a man climbs into a woman's French horn and disappears,

an infant is born from under a T-shirt
and turns into a squalling viola.
Waves of laughter and applause crash across the concert hall.
Responding violinists prance like stilted willets

who sawed pine dusted horse tails
across silver strings
to make sunny surf sounds
and Mozart fun.

# Sonata: Monterey Peninsula
as sung to me by Arcangelo Corelli



*for Jack Gray, Mary Jo Wade, Sam and Meg*

1.   Preludio/Largo

Deep off this peninsula a canyon drops
under the Pacific, the wet edge
of a continental mountain range.

In it plankton spin as whales cruise through.
Between these extremes, there's most of life.
Protozoa and mammals flank

vast varieties of plants, fish and birds.
This life wells up like evolution
toward the coast, casting ashore

broken kelp, sea lions, shells and gulls.
Beaches receive these like an invasion
liberating rocks and sand.

The land accepts its role as surf
makes sand and foam around
and around in whirlpool

waves that sculpt rocks.

2.    Allemanda/Allegro

Bottlebrown sea palms bow under seas,
as kelp heads mimic sea otters rolled
on their backs to picnic on their chests.

Pelicans gulp below waves
like pterodactyls that grew plastic bags on their chins
by robbing from a fish store on the wharf.

Below golden kelp pennants
and the silver upside down sea, otters climb
down kelp stalks to abalones that cling

to rockbacks at the feet of kelp.
Above, a heron bobs on sea legs
balanced on a floating log

and stabs water flashes for a fish.

3.    Sarabanda/Largo

These grand canyons undersea
and this pine and cypress-gripped shore
rain and drain on each other

in a system that runs
air and water together into one
gigantic liquid atmosphere.

Life responded with a variety show,
homegrown talent of folk art
to share each stage.

Bat rays, starry flounder and sandabs
repeat what the huge halibut does best,
just as black-necked stilts, avocets and willets

imitate the dowitcher. A good act
seems worth maybe a dozen tries.
Nature scribbles new inventions as it sorts

flaws and favors for a breakthrough.
This seacanyon and headland cry out:
gulls sit on fences or find mossy nooks

when wind chokes their gullets with a storm,
but scream like cats with white wings,
a piercing fish gut yodel that can be heard

above the loudest surf. On rocks cut off
by ocean blows, sealions bellow challenges
to their tribe. All day they sing basso continuo

and bark to defy the noisy ocean that never ceases
till they dive below to bite at perch
that school before their eyes like sailing mobiles

full of switching yellow tails.

4.   Giga/Allegro

To these I add my voice and make
words, not love, to resound back
at this overwhelming ocean.

I'm like those scuba divers
who back into surf, waves against
their wet suits, to enter the other world

that covers most of this one,
that we came from, that got us ready,
by teaching us to take air along,

for our longer dives in space.
Now, with Monterey our anchor,
with a new aquarium bringing sea life ashore,

we're ready to explore
coastal canyons that rift
down through the continental shelf

from light to life to abyssal plain,
from sound to silent soundings,
from bird dart flung at flash

to the diatom suck of baleen whales,
from orange and black monarch butterfly sunned
in Pacific Grove to chambered nautilus

that drops into sea canyons like a moon.

# A poet is like Tevfik Esenc, exile

farmer, eighty-two years old,
the only person left on Earth
who speaks Oubykh, a Caucasian tongue.

There are over eighty phonemes, including three
ways to say "shhh." There are eighty-two
consonants, only three vowels,
which must twist Tevfik's tongue.

Oubykh is a treasure chest of sounds!
whose decline began in 1864
when Moslem herders and farmers were driven
from Russia after the Crimean War.

Oubykhs learned Turkish to survive
resettlement in Ottoman Turkey
near the Sea of Marmara
in Tevfik's village of Bandirma.

"No one is responsible
for the death of our mother tongue.
It happened because of our poverty,
and our being dispersed several times

by Russian Czars and the Turks,"
said Tevfik speaking Turkish
through an interpreter, since no one
could translate spoken Oubykh.

Esenc like a poet has gone on four tours
to Oslo and Paris to speak to linguists
and be recorded. When Tevfik dies
a peoples' memory fades to a dead tongue

like the swollen tongue of a whale
that goes back up into the mountains
to the oldest center of Europe:
the Caucasus valleys east of the Black Sea.

Some tribes became the first Europeans
by escaping there from the dangerous crossroads
of the Middle East way back when both Europe
and Asia were unpeopled and unnamed.

Only one hundred fifty years ago
fifty thousand spoke Oubykh,
that complicated river of sounds
that ran among herds and farms down

to the Black Sea. Now, Tevfik stands
like one tree in history, still
soaking up wet sounds in roots
torn from ancient human ground.

Esenc is a farmer with an invisible barn
full of organic jewels as he speaks
in Bandirma, on the south coast of Marmara
south of Constantinople/Istanbul,

too near the capital to keep
Oubykh alive. Tevfik is like most of us,
a displaced person, uprooted,
too far along to return where we came from,

too wise to know where we are going,
as our tongues learn to say
new foreign combinations
every day.